CATHOLIC GIRL

Poems by

Elsie Johnstone

Selected poems

by

Elsie (Allen) Johnstone

Catholic girl
Copyright © 2020 by Elsie Johnstone
978-0-6488619-6-6

Published by G. & E. Johnstone. All rights reserved. No part of this publication may be reproduced in any manner whatsoever, or stored in a retrieval system or transmitted in any form or by any means, electronic, mechanical, photocopying, recording or otherwise, without the prior written permission of the author, except in the case of brief quotations embodied in critical articles or reviews. Please do not participate in or encourage the piracy of copyrighted materials in violation of authors' rights. Purchase only authorized editions.

The publisher and author assume no responsibility or liability whatsoever on the behalf of any purchaser or reader of this material. Any perceived slight of specific people or organizations is unintentional. While all attempts have been made to verify information provided in this publication, neither the author nor the publisher assumes any responsibility for errors, omissions or contrary interpretation of the subject matter herein.

Catholic girl is also available as an e-book for Kindle, Kobo, Apple and other devices.

Dedication

To my brother John, deceased, who devoted his life as a Catholic Priest to ministering to others, preaching the Church's message, creating community for newcomers to this country and the poor and displaced and, through his kind nature and good humour, leading others to live good and productive lives. His was a lonely and dutiful life. How much more fulfilling would it have been with a soulmate by his side?

To my baby brother Robert, deceased, who had the promise of a bright future brutally taken away from him at the age of twelve years, and who continued his life journey trying his best to deal with the sin that had been committed against him. He suffered a slow death for forty years, until he could do it no more. My heart breaks for him.

Contents

Introduction 1

Catholic Girl 3
Sin 4
Transubstantiation 5
Catholic words 6
The Nine First Fridays 7
Hell 8
AMDG 9
Holy Water 10
Limbo 11
Sex and marriage 12
What would Jesus think? 13
The little wooden church 14
Meeting place 15
Burn 16
Mass on Sunday 18
Saying the Rosary 20
Classified Catholics 21
How many angels can stand on the head of a pin? 22
Thief in the night 24
Lapsed Catholic 25
Jesus the politician 26
Conscience 27
Where does the buck stop? 28
Bad apples 29
Father John 30

Occasions of sin	32
The guru	33
The truth about truth	34
Religion and football	35
Drugs in sport	37
Eighteen	38
Misogyny	40
Why?	41
Jim	42
Julia	44
Midwinter madness	46
Boys will be boys	48
Go to Hell, George Pell	49
Suffer little children	50
Betrayed	52
Bless me, Father	54
Out of options	56
Black lives matter	57
ANZAC Day 2020	58
Cleaning out the garage	60
Summer 2020	62
Locked out of the sunshine	63
Groundhog day	64
Other works by Elsie Johnstone	67

Introduction

We are a product of our times. In my lifetime, I have seen religion drift from being central to society to a place where it has almost faded from the national consciousness.

The poems in this book signpost my journey from a devoted Catholic daughter who attended Mass each Sunday for thirty years, had children baptised and attend Catholic schools, contributed to the planned giving program and helped organise and participate in fund-raising functions, to someone full of disappointment and disillusion. Trust has been broken.

When one of my three brothers became a priest, I had a chance to see the Church from the inside. I loved my brother but I had grown up with him and I knew his faults as well as his good points. He was one of us; no more or less special than me or my siblings, yet that is not what he was told. I came to realise that the Church is a misogynistic boys' club that excludes half the population from the hierarchy.

While discussing theology and the Church's teachings with my brother, he suggested I seek enlightenment by reading Saint Thomas Aquinas, a 13th century Dominican monk. I did and wasn't impressed! Aquinas spent a considerable portion of his God-given life organizing angels into groups and pondering how many could stand on the head of a pin. I lapsed.

A lapsed Catholic is one who remains a cultural Catholic while tolerating the Church's inconsistencies and idiosyncrasies.

Then my youngest brother revealed a horrible truth, that our family had been betrayed by the institution we had lived our lives by. He had been raped by a priest at the age of 12. My brother had tried to tell my father but he was rebuked, so kept his secret from the family until eighteen months before he committed suicide, forty trauma-filled years of strained relationships, counselling and drug and alcohol abuse later.

Our family sacrificed two brothers to the institution that is the Catholic Church. One went freely and did good things. He chose that life and I am proud of the way he lived. But the other brother's life was brutally taken from him and then this act of bastardry was covered up while the perpetrators went onto ruin more lives.

The poems in this book document my journey from believer, to benevolent doubter, to lapsed Catholic and then to where I am now, full of disillusionment, disgust and mistrust.

In Australia, religion, football and politics are intertwined and basically operate on similar premises. That's why you will also find a sprinkling of poems about football and politics in here as well. Enjoy!

Catholic girl

A Catholic girl learns when growing up
There are rules for everything
They are there to control you
Absolve you, send your soul to Heaven
Keep you away from occasions of sin
There are rules for when you are wed
As well as rules for when you are dead
Do good, avoid evil
Pray hard, reject the devil
This simple mantra is at the religion's core
Just be careful what you wish for
One thing we know for an absolute fact
Is our conscience dictates the way that we act
However, if our neighbours' goods we purloin
Remember, there are two sides to every coin
It's not always your fault if you do great harm
So if you sin be not alarmed
Blame the temporal consequences of original sin
Individuals are not responsible for the state we're in
If you go to confession to be absolved
All your problems will be resolved

Sin

A good Catholic girl
Knows all about sin
There are sins that are called venial
Which are quite small and menial
Mortal sins are more serious by far
Murder, missing Mass, eating meat on Friday, stealing a car
Pride, envy, gluttony, lust, anger, sloth and greed
Are the seven deadly sins, very serious indeed
But the most serious of all, as far as I can tell
Are carnal sins that send you straight to hell

Transubstantiation

In holy Mass at the consecration
We confront the ultimate mystery
Of transubstantiation
Bread and wine is changed
Spiced, sliced, diced
Rearranged
Until it becomes the body and blood of Christ
With this promise eternal life is sold
Keep trust, the precious faith uphold
But, pray take time to consider this
What if bread and wine is substituted
With Coca-Cola and potato chips?
Would transubstantiation be disputed?

Catholic words

I have a posse of words I will take to my grave
Taught to me so my soul would be saved
These are the words that set us Catholics apart
Words that are indelibly etched into the heart
In any given crowd if said out loud and clear
Any other Catholic standing near
Will look at you and the truth unfurl
You are simply a good Catholic girl
Plenary Indulgence, Advent, Adultery
Angelus, Holy Water, Acolyte, Blasphemy
Apostles' Creed, Novena, Canonization
Antichrist, Eucharist, Beatification
Benediction, Repentance, Immaculate Conception
Canon Law, Eternal Life, Resist Temptation
Annulment, Celibacy, Excommunication
Penance for Sins, Transubstantiation
Examine your Conscience, Annunciate
It's a dreadful Sin to Masturbate
Faith, believe, obey the Ten Commandments
Repent, kneel and pray, don't forget your Penance
This dictionary of Catholic words I unconsciously compiled
As an innocent and impressionable child

The Nine First Fridays

At home in our house displayed high on the wall
A picture of the Sacred Heart, blood, veins and all
Scary to look at, gave us youngsters a fright
Especially if you were home alone in the night
Catholics firmly believed in the Sacred Heart
The icon gave us hope and set us apart
The notion of this devotion came from Saint Margaret Alacoque
Whose life was lived devoid of pleasure, so joyless and stark
She claimed she received a sacred vision
From the Virgin, who prescribed a mission
To enlist believers to hear Mass on Nine First Fridays of each month
This achieved, we believed our tickets would be punched
On the day of our death when toting sin and repentance
We would be guaranteed the honour of heavenly acceptance
So, with this bribe in mind every year in January
Young hopeful souls began the First Friday journey
While school was in, the nuns reminded us and it was fine
But come holidays, it completely slipped the mind
All cosy in bed we'd forget all about it
Too late we would realise our First Friday plan was flouted
And we were back to the very beginning
To start the Nine Fridays all over again
Our efforts doomed, no hope of winning
Every year of our school life it was always the same
We never did quite achieve the First Friday goal
Of being free to sin without considering the toll

Hell

Hell is an interesting place
Built for sinners, whatever your race
Down there you burn right through to your core
Your suffering is great, you writhe on the floor
You lament loudly as you push through the pain
"Oh, if I only had my life over again
I'd repent and I'd sin no more!"
But your lot is cast, you are beyond redemption
You have missed your one chance at Heaven
That's where God is with his heavenly creatures
A peaceful place with wonderful features
Live your life always aiming to be there
Beware false prophets, they are everywhere
They try to ensnare us earthly creatures
Take our money, feed false gospel, pretend to be preachers

AMDG

School blazers, school jumpers, hats and school ties
Defined us as a group in townspeople's eyes
Identified us with the school we attended
Whether from Irish or English we'd descended
Our school should be there to educate and refine us
Unfortunately, it also was inclined to define us
As Protestant or Catholic dogs
Sitting on logs
Eating maggots out of frogs
To one camp or the other we were assigned
Deeply loved by our own but by others maligned
One trick we Catholics had over the Devil
Was AMDG written on each page in the middle
Before we'd start our work each day
We'd rule a line on our page and pray
"Ad Maiorem Dei Gloriam"
For God's greater glory
And whether it was maths or writing a story
Our work became spiritually meritorious
No matter how bad or inglorious
The work on the page was
It didn't matter because
God would fix it and make it better
He was our own personal phototypesetter

Holy Water

Fill my font with Holy Water
Sprinkle me with fear
With the hyssop brush splash the masses
So the Devil won't come near
Let's be like St Teresa of Avila
When confronted with the abominable one
She prayed aloud for protection from evil
Deliverance from the Devil
Also known as Satan's son
But he sensed her fear and returned
Unconcerned that he'd been spurned
She flung Holy Water in desperation
Then celebration, great elation
The beast was slain
Never to bother her again
No longer the formidable one
So how do you make this wonderful stuff, this Holy Water?
This recipe came directly from the Bishop's daughter
She said, 'Forget the blessings and all that shit
Simply put water in a pressure cooker and boil the hell out of it!'

Limbo

Limbo's that place between Heaven and Purgatory
Where the sight of God in all his glory
Is denied to the heathen who's not been baptised
Whose fate is irreversible, cannot be revised
Because once you arrive there
Your future is sealed. You can't go anywhere
For all eternity. You must stay in that place
Hanging out with nothing to do, far away from God's grace
That is why it was important to baptise a child
As soon as possible in case he dies, unreconciled
And with Original Sin still on his soul
Forever damned to that celestial black hole
Where there is no hope or chance of reprieve
A curse handed down from Adam and Eve
When they ate the apple and sinned in the garden
The whole race condemned, devoid of God's pardon
And that is why, on the sly, I always poured water
On any son or daughter, whose soul was besmirched
Because he had yet to be churched
In my childish mind I'd rationalise
The baby was reprieved if baptised
And could go to Heaven in case of death
So we left behind would not feel so bereft

Sex and marriage

I learnt all I know about carnal knowledge
From the learned men at Cardinal's College
They said every woman is an occasion of sin
I am wicked if I give into him
The woman does not own her body
And if by chance we make a baby
I have no right to make a choice
Abortion out of the question, I have no voice
Unmarried pregnancy brings great shame
The man is never to blame
Instead, girls stay chaste until you marry
If tempted, cross your legs, think of Mary
Procreation is not for recreation
So right up to the wedding reception
Resist his urging, stay a virgin
Take your lead from the Immaculate Conception
Choose your husband very carefully
Marriage is for life and happy family
Divorce is simply not on the table
Pray to God, forgive your man, if you are able
However, if in the end you don't get fulfilment
You can always settle for an annulment
Pretend the union never existed
That you never coexisted, have the marriage delisted

What would Jesus think?

What would Jesus Christ say
If he was around today
Would he kneel down and pray
To deliver his people from unspeakable evil?
What would Jesus Christ do
About the lack of people in the pew
Would he say he always knew
Bad apples would his truth undo?
What would Jesus Christ want
From the priest at the Baptismal font
Who rejected the First Commandment
To love one another with good intent
What would Jesus Christ need
From followers of his ancient creed
Would he want to intercede
To sort the good seed from the weed
What could Jesus Christ expect
From those who made themselves a sect
That rejects and shows no respect
For half the race, the other sex
Does Jesus Christ see a future
For those who protected the abuser
Rejected the victim who was left to suffer
The shame that was not theirs to claim
I think he would be so terribly sad
That those who should know better, could be so bad

The little wooden church

The little wooden church stood proudly in the centre of town
Weekdays silent, but come Sunday crowds milled 'round
For community prayer in this meeting place
To praise the Lord and gain God's grace
And afterwards when that was done
To meet and gather in the sun
To discuss the people that mattered to them
The past week's events and how they viewed them
This little wooden church was a community project
Built without the aid of an exclusive architect
The faithful thought it important that they had their own place
To worship, so they bought the land to build on this space
The faithful congregation toiled to put it there
Provided free wood and labour when they had time to spare
The building was a humble place but so too, were they
They didn't build a monument; they built a place to pray
This simple wooden structure is more pleasing to God by far
Than any flash cathedral, no matter how five star

Meeting place

Past the lights, south of the highway
There's a place where people come to pray
At Save Our Mortal Souls, they praise our saviour
Practice religion, celebrate life in Australia
At Sunday Mass the sea of faces
Represents a multitude of races
It's a community hub where people can come
To worship, sing and pray as one
Where they celebrate from whence they came
What makes them different and how they're the same
A welcoming place where all nations gather
Reach out, pray, laugh and chatter
And share hardships and triumphs in prayer
They feel at home here, more than anywhere
But then a man with a large red hat
Decided that their little church was just that
Too free and happy, open and welcoming
He wanted a building that was far more imposing
Their wonderful meeting place, they'd built from their labours
Saved and fund raised, worked alongside their neighbours
Was to be replaced with an ecclesiastical monument
Devoid of community, love, hope and sentiment
The spirit has gone, the Sunday numbers are down
People don't gather when the church bells sound
The new church is a shrine to vanity
To replace the old church, was criminal insanity

Burn

Notre Dame, mother of God
Fuelled by dogma, centuries old
Wild fire, smoke belching
Gritty truths squelching
Embers tumbling to a glowing hole
Where absolute truth once stood
Now reduced to mere burning wood

Wherein once sacred relics burn
To reach a point of no return
Beyond emotion, beyond words, beyond tears
The people speak, no one hears

Notre Dame, mother good
What augurs for the mortal soul
Now that nought remains but a deep black hole
Will you survive? Be revived?
To live and thrive?

Notre Dame mother of gold
And dubious wealth, the bell has tolled
Your shallow shell for all exposed
Trinkets and treasures transposed
To a demolition site

Notre Dame, mother of mothers
Cry for the child violated
For his sisters and brothers
Be angry for parents betrayed
While the hypocritical priests prayed
Apportioning blame and showing no shame
The flames spew out with hypocrisy
Into the gaping ash-hole where truth should be
The tide has turned, your power relinquished
The fires out, our faith extinguished

Mass on Sunday

In my Sunday best dress of cherry red
Fluffy white beret on my head
Black patent shoes, white socks, very quaint
A vision of innocence, a little saint
My sisters dressed just like me
A credit to our family tree
Mum looking very schlick
Pretty dress, bright lipstick
Gazes lovingly at us, her life's work
Proud of her knitting and needlework
There was no denying we are very cute
Says Dad all scrubbed up in his wedding suit
He is proud of his family as we make our way
To Mass on a Sunday, but we weren't there just to pray
There were other good reasons for going to Mass
Not that you'd mention it, for that would be crass
After the Latin was interned and sermon delivered
We'd adjourn for a cuppa and for all things considered
Catch up with the gossip, see how others were going

The cows they were milking, what grain they were sowing
Had Arthur had any luck with the fishing up the lake
How was business going, who made this delicious cake?
How was the widower Tom coping all alone
Did old Annie feel safer now she had the phone
Why was the town prostitute singing in the choir
Was she merely pumping up organs of desire
Was the bank manager still dallying with the teller
Had his wife forgiven him, did anybody tell her
What about the footy team
Weren't they doing good
Did you hear that there'd been
Another robbery in the 'hood
If the mob from Melbourne buy the general store
It's the thin edge of the wedge, there will be uproar
Then the priest would join the milling crowd
To be heartily congratulated out loud
For the brilliant sermon that he gave
The potential souls he may have saved
Conversation adopts a religious bent
A spiritual aura, of love and good intent
It always altered the conversation
When the priest joined in with the congregation

Saying the Rosary

Every night straight after tea the family would say the Rosary
We kids did it reluctantly, but without a fuss
We'd all kneel and pray, it was expected of us
It was something my parents did every single day
They structured their time and lived their lives that way
The Rosary is a sort of meditative chant
So boringly repetitious, we'd incant and incant
The same words over and over, all in unison
A conductor and his band of musicians
We young ones were more interested in rock 'n' roll
At every chance we had we would find a loophole
To rescue us from spending time on our knees
No excuse was good enough, despite all our pleas
The Rosary would drone on and on
Glory Be to the Father and to the Son
Then the Our Father and many Hail Marys
Our eyes would glaze over
We were away with the fairies
By then, Mum had entered a meditative sleep
Dad had his hands full trying to keep
Our minds on our prayer, keeping us there
Finally, at last we'd get to the end
Our knees were locked up, we couldn't bend
We'd come alive and quickly make our escape
To do homework, play music, watch television
Why insist that the Rosary be our mission
When we could easily have said it by audiotape

Classified Catholics

Like the great Aquinas who categorised angels on a pin
I have spent a bit of time categorising Catholics and their kin
There are various classes of Catholic, we're not all the same
Starting with the mighty leaders who live in the Vatican
We women can never aspire to that, so the most that we can hope
Is to be a committed Catholic who walks the walk, more faithful than the Pope
Women have small Catholic folk who are born into the religion
Baptised as little babies into the Catholic Christian tradition
Then comes the student Catholic, indoctrinated through the schools
Where a child learns all the dogma and how to follow church rules
This often morphs into the cultural Catholic where life is viewed through the prism
Of a person who doesn't know what he thinks and can't make a decision
So becomes a wishy-washy Catholic, dictated to by sacred rites
Goes to church at holy times and does business with the Southern Cross Knights
Lapsed Catholics tend to neglect rules but stay within the fold
Taking comfort from the option to repent when they get old
Disaffected Catholics are not Catholics any more
They can be disregarded when I add up the total score
I calculate six stages and you may agree or disagree
It's a perfunctory effort on my behalf, and that's all it's meant to be

How many angels can stand on the head of a pin?

Saint Thomas Aquinas spent his life wondering
Exactly how many angels can stand on a pin
It's a useless question that gets you right in
'Cos it doesn't matter what the answer is
The chance is, it doesn't mean a thing
Angels are spiritual creatures in a physical universe
So the calculation is difficult, or worse
It can't be worked out
Without some element of doubt
How many angels can stand on the head of a pin?
It's such a silly question, where to begin
A whole host of seraphim, the highest ranked of all
They are God's favourites so they won't be allowed to fall
Perhaps one little cherub, cutely round and squat
He might bring his little mate along, as an afterthought
Two big archangels each flapping just one wing
Pivoting extra carefully so good tidings they can bring
A bevy of fallen angels tumbling all about
Sticking pins into the guards who strove to drive them out

A couple of loving cupids playing on their harps
Two's company, three's a crowd, don't dare tear them apart
Three angels of death
'Cos death always comes in threes
They will prick you with the pin so you will catch disease
Beautiful cherubim won't be wasting time
As God's faithful attendants, they're too busy to have downtime
A group of guardian angels so sweet and so small
Wondering what they are doing. Should they be there at all?
In fact, if we take time to work on this equation
Why stop at angels for this ceremonial occasion
Nuns are such lovely pious things
How many of them and how many pins?
The good priest, the bad priest,
the monk who practices what he preaches
The rabbi, the imam, the guru, and the swami
If I pinned them, could that amount to blasphemy
Then there's the street angels and home devils
That fit would be wrong on many different levels
I have realised that this is a useless exercise
When it's all boiled down and calculations done
It matters not whether the answer is a million or is one

Thief in the night

Don't blame me for being a hedonist
Instead, lay the blame on the evangelists
Who preached this message when we were young
Don't get too complacent out there in the sun
For you know not the day nor the hour
When everything will turn rank and sour
You will be scrutinised, criticized and chastised
Your life will be closed, your sins exposed
You'll be off to Hell, or at the very least, Purgatory
A sad, sad story, no guts no glory
Death comes like a thief in the night
Live a life of virtue like God's shining knight
Death jumps upon you when you least expect it
Aim to be blameless, try to perfect it
Hunker down, pray and do good works
Then you too, will enjoy all of God's perks
Unfortunately, my child's brain took it the wrong way
I vowed and declared that from that very day
I would live each hour as if it was my last
Enjoy each moment, savour each repast
Never worry about sin and repentance
I can add that to my ultimate sentence
When I turn up before the pearly gates
And my ledger is tallied and I am given my rates
In case of a breach of warranty
And the whole thing is a huge conspiracy
A bird in the hand is worth two in the bush
Enjoy everything now before shove comes to push

Lapsed Catholic

Being a Catholic is so overrated
Now I am lapsed, I feel liberated
No longer rules and doctrine to adhere to
Or celibate men telling me what to do
My belief system has collapsed
My religion is lapsed
Indoctrination of the child
Took years and years to recompile
Now I live my life in style
Enjoying autonomy while
Respecting my own thoughts
Doing as I ought
Without the constraints
Of the Church and her saints
Lapsed, lapsed, lapsed, what does it mean
It means I'm divorced from the Catholic machine
Lapsed, lapsed, lapsed, how does that look
Instead of Mass on Sunday, I now read a book
Lapsed, lapsed, lapsed, how does that feel
I'm liberated from my Achilles heel, the Holy Seal
Lapsed, Lapsed, lapsed, what can I do
Whatever I judge right, whatever I want to

Jesus the politician

Jesus' father was a carpenter, a tradie at heart
It was expected that his son would follow him, given that sort of start
He could have even been a tiler, a plumber or an electrician
But he chose to do none of that, he became a politician
In the war-torn Middle East
Which has rarely enjoyed the gift of peace
He wandered the lakes of Galilee, preaching to the throngs
His left wing socialist view of the world, sorting right from wrongs
"All things on earth are not just for you
They are to be shared with your neighbours too
Doesn't matter if you are Jew or Gentile
An emperor, a king, or plain rank and file
A Palestinian, Arab, Roman or Persian
I do good deeds and attend your needs
I fix you if you are hurting
Love is all l have and I give it with a full heart
You too can play the same game, it is not too late to start
I cleared the temple of thieves, thugs and power brokers
The modern day bikies, bankers and self-promoters
Take care of your fellow man, every one's a neighbour
Do good in the face of harm, forgiveness is your saviour
Turn the other cheek to those who hate you
Forgive those who persecute and berate you."
Standing with the downtrodden against the entrenched conventional school
It was never his intention to be socially cool
If Jesus walked the earth today there's no doubt he'd denounce
Rich men squeezing the poor, wanting more, leaving not an ounce

Conscience

I am on a voyage of self-discovery
To find out who I really am
There's a self out there, some other othery
Am I true to her or am I sham?
If I put in effort and show persistence
Display commitment and resilience
The final effect may be somewhere deep inside I discover
That waiting there for me to uncover
Is somebody much nicer than me
And if that's the real me
What does that make me?
An imposter, the seeker or the seekee?
What if there's no real me lurking
And I am not that better person?
Is it my conscience telling me
To accept who I am and not who I want to be
Be true to myself, take responsibility
It's up to me how I live my life
Don't threaten me with the afterlife
Will finding myself end in tears
Will I lose myself midst the babble of peers
Become the clothes that I wear or the titles I carry
The money I make or the person I marry?
Live your life knowing the real dinky-di you
The sum of your past, present and future too
Be proud, project towards the self you wish to be
The only one, the truly uniquely me

Where does the buck stop?

Written in 2013, when an AFL team, Essendon Football Club was immersed in a scandal where, in order to win games, young men were injected with drugs at the whim of leaders of the club. At the time, the team motto was, "Whatever it takes"!

Where does the buck stop
When the rot sets in?
James Hird, the board, or the pharmacy king?
Corruption, gambling, drug use
Maverick scientists free to abuse
Come inside we have nothing to hide
Vitamin booster injections
Increase statistical projections
Take this for strength and conditioning
Don't be frightened it's only a vitamin
Forget the obligation of duty of care
Come last day in September, we want to be there
Indemnify the club, a form here to sign
Just in case we have gone over the line
What of the coaches and duty of care
Who were they concerned for, were they aware?
In their ruthless pragmatism they used naïve young men
Ethical margins reduced time and again

Bad apples

Two good apples hanging on a tree
One bad apple came along and then there was three
Three bad apples hanging by the door
A good apple joins the gang and then there were four
We know that one bad apple at the bottom of the pile
Can spoil all the other apples in less than a little while
Bad apples have once been good apples that become rotten
That good apples shouldn't mix with bad, shouldn't be forgotten
If with scumbags, creeps and paedos you hangout
You are likely to grow like the friends that you care about
Corruption is ultimately corruptive
Fear of losing the upper-hand destructive
Anything goes as long as no one knows
It's important that you understand
That the standard you wander past
Is the sum of the cards you hold in your hand

Father John

What has happened to Father John
His body is dead, his soul has gone
Does he live on and on?
In that microsecond between life and death
As Father John breathed his final breath
It became apparent
Transparent
The ultimate truth did unfold
Unfortunately, it can't be told
Until, that day
It is our turn to pass away
And then, we will confront the mystery
Of our ultimate history

Where has Father John gone?
His body has been anointed
Will his dear soul live on and on and on?
Or will he be disappointed
Something for us to reflect upon

Did a band of celestial creatures
Whose job it is to welcome preachers
Embrace John and grant his reward
For all the sacrifices he'd endured?
Was he met at Heaven's door
By all his folk who'd gone before?
Did his spirit soar and soar?
Did at last he enjoy
What he'd been promised as a boy
And lived his life accordingly
So that the face of God he'd see

And yet ...

Could it be that John finally knew
That his world-view was quite untrue
That after life there is a void
At death his hopes and dreams destroyed
There is nothing else, we live and die
When we breathe our last, it is "Goodbye."

Occasions of sin

At first a baby eats what the mother feeds her
She has no say, no one asks if it pleases her
But, as soon as that baby has some say
She lets you know; she spits it away
Eat it up, it's good for you, come, eat it up, enjoy your stew
Not on your life, it tastes like poo!
It is never ice cream or chocolate that is refused
It's always carrots, broccoli or leek that's reproduced
A baby chooses her diet, no matter how much our entreating
She'll eat what she likes, without fear of displeasing
Why do we lose ability to do what we choose
To tread our own path, be able to refuse
Without oversight from a higher authority
Who wears the mantle of moral superiority
I ask why is it that almost everything we like to do
Is considered by the thought police to be taboo
Don't eat that, it gives you diabetes
Don't put sugar on your Weeties
Don't use butter on your bread
Spread foul-tasting margarine instead

Don't eat that
It will make you fat
Spuds are bad for you
But sweet potatoes will do
Watch the calories, go for a run
Life has to be hard, we're not here for fun
Sex is bad, your bodies are evil
To masturbate is the work of the devil
Bad thoughts should be driven from your head
Say a quick prayer to the Virgin instead
Don't question, be humble, be always obedient
Beware occasions of sin or you may become deviant
Don't hang out with that person, don't be a brat
Everything is black or white, don't forget that
There are no shades of grey, just right and wrong
Do what we tell you if you wish to belong
Rule makers are expected their own rules to follow
For words without actions are hard to swallow
It's all very well to take high moral ground
But in life, the hypocrite quickly becomes uncrowned

The guru

Narcissist guru likes to criticise
Tell you he is viewing you through other people's eyes
"The way you sup your soup
Is altogether so uncouth
Just letting you know the score
So you won't do it anymore."
Criticisms disguised as helpful advice
Leading you on, telling you lies
Then the isolation process begins
Separating you from family and friends
Telling you things that just aren't true
Gets you in a knot so you don't know what to do
A Guru displays selfish and unreliable behaviour
While always pretending to be your saviour
Forgets arrangements, always late for any date
Has you doubting your judgement, accepting your fate
You have overreacted, been distracted, punishment contacted
It won't happened again, but it does
Death by a thousand different cuts
Narcissistic gurus are self-obsessed, evil to be around
Keep away from them, leave them where they're found
They repeat their behaviours over and over
Damage innocent people who never recover

The truth about truth

When is a truth not true?
When is it not genuine or actual
Can it be a personal truth
Does it always have to be factual?
What is the difference between truth and fact
And does it even matter
Do the two ever interact?
Should you always speak your mind, avoiding idle chatter
A fact is a universally acknowledged truth
That fact becomes reality is never in dispute
Truths can be created or discovered
Whereas reality is truth waiting to be uncovered
And is always the same for you as it is for me
It has nothing to do with power; it's about authenticity
Truth relies on facts and facts can sometimes be disproved
Then, the essence of truth is subsequently removed
If a truth is not true, it is a lie, an alternative fact, fake news
And power seekers often use it to excuse, bemuse, abuse
Truth is removed from faith which in reality is trust
Trust can be broken so faith does not work for all of us
One can repeat, reassert, reword, purport
Until your face is blue
If truth hasn't reality as support
That makes it quite untrue

Religion and football

At the high altar they stand
Preaching their truths from their own grandstand
Two men exalted above the rest.
The Priest consecrated to God, a sage, the best
The Football Coach because he can tell us
How to play the game to win the premiership chalice
On sacred ground they stand and expound
This place they love best, their home ground
The Priest calls his team to prayer
The Coach talks psychological warfare
Preaching profoundly to tribes of warriors
Each one adorned in bright club colours
Fire and blood, energy, power and passion
Imparting a message of hope in his fashion
"Listen to me, hear my words and you will not fail
Follow me as we seek and find the Holy Grail
Fight the battles well and you will make this team
Just do whatever it takes, if you see what I mean."
Team members listen to these men who know all things
About the game plan and the ultimate reward it brings
There's no place for sheilas in this running game
But blood spilt for the team brings sky-high acclaim
Put your body on the line, by thirty-three you're done
At that same age, God sacrificed Jesus, his only son
Dogma dictates what truths must be sold
The ritual describes how the game will unfold
The similarities are significant, football and religion are not so different

Drugs in sport

Lance Armstrong's not Aussie
It doesn't happen here
Never fear
We are not the same
Our athletes are squeaky clean
Ahead of the game
Ignore lines we have crossed
Disregarding the cost
To young men with stents taped onto an arm
Or saline drips inserted into a vein
No harm
Whatever it takes to win the game
Train in high altitude
So oxygen depletes them
Give athletes fresh aptitude
And others can't defeat them
Radical surgery
Mends that broken knee
Diet, training, recovery meticulously scrutinized
All things analysed
Alarm bells ringing
Bookies singing
Young men turned into cattle to be traded and bought
Media barons now own our sport
Turned it into business, couldn't care less
When the fans protest
"We own it, we invest!"

Eighteen

Take my precious son
My job is done
He is highly skilled at kicking a ball
But he is just a boy, hasn't lived at all
Nevertheless, he is desperate to go
And who am I to tell him no
He has been dreaming of this moment since he was a kid
This culminates everything he did
To ensure that he was strong, skilled and quick to the ball
All he ever wanted to do was to play football
How he played the game was the ultimate test
The score was irrelevant if you gave it your best
He honoured the sport considered it pure
A test of character and human nature
Then at sport's grand altar on the other side of the nation
They exposed his young body to modification
Styled him and filed him
Reviled and beguiled him

Will you do whatever it takes in 2013?
Push to the last even though it is hurting
Moving on, training hard
Going that extra mile, that one final yard
Looking forward to the new season
Whatever it takes, beyond all reason
On-going search to increase performance
Utmost compliance, player conformance
Medically aggressive, push the edge
Do what it takes, the ultimate message
The rules of sport irreverently discard
If it gives an edge, an extra yard
It's all worth it, son. It's not that hard
Disregard how wrong it feels
We must honour our sponsorship deals
Loopholes are simply there to be found
You must grind your opponent into the ground
Don't think of the future, it's all in the now
Young health bodies sacrificed to sacred money cow

Misogyny

This is our son that we begun
Home spun
Protected, perfected and socially connected
Our grown up boy
Pride and joy
Side by side
We taught him to empathize
Walk the walk
Not talk the talk
Find solutions
For wayward emotions
Communicate
Put himself in another's place
Treat people with respect
And yet he's sexist
He joins in the hype
Lampoons the stereotype
With sexual vilification
Of the leader of our nation
Because she's woman and not man
Where did we go wrong?

Why?

Why do I have empathy
With live meat trade sheep
While what happens to our refugees
Doesn't bother me
Why do I have sympathy
For the great white whale
While men imprisoned on Manus
Are treated reprehensively
Why do we fail to see
Our differences do not define us
As alien others
Refugees are like you and me
Write down white supremacy
Instead share our humanity
We are all one, you and me
Why do we feel no shame
For policy made in our name
That disregards empathy
Shows no sympathy
For asylum seeker pain

Jim

Men from Australia convinced our Da
Jim could be rich, a big football star
Mam was against it, cried all day
"He's just a lad. We can't send him away
At eighteen years old, the lad is so vulnerable
He could get into drugs and drink too much alcohol."
Da saw Jim's chance to make his name
Be paid good money for playing a game
"Our lad has talent. We can't stand in his way
There is no future for him playing GAA."
Jim's going left a huge gap in the family
Changing it forever irrevocably
One pair less football boots at the back doorway
One less coat, gloves and scarf in the hallway
Around the table one empty place
His absence leaving a gaping space
Each Sunday evening Jim called home
Uniting his family in Ballyroan
Shrill ring announcing Jim's weekly call
Like army drill, we all rushed to the hall
Lined up on the stairs and waited our turn to speak
To tell our big brother the news of the week
Da talked first about sport and men's business
Then it was Mam's turn for local news interest
All about weather, wind, hail and rain
Have you been to Mass? Hope you've not been drinking again

Ah, Jimmy we all love you and we all miss you
I'll hand you over to your brothers and sisters
Jim's team won through to finals in September
The family travelled to watch the game
A truly grand trip they all remember
His team lost, Jim was to blame
Ran across the mark, was how they described it
"How the feck would he know that?" Da adamantly decried it
The fans still loved Jim, so continued celebrations
Forgave our hero, who was loved in both nations
Ma missed Jim. It broke her heart
"Mothers don't have sons to live twelve thousand miles apart"
The family grew and left Ballyroan
Only Mam and Da took the Sunday phone home
Talked of family and Jim's lovely wife
The youth foundation to which he devoted his life
One November night, rain blowing off Atlantic Ocean
"I'm to fight the battle of my life," Jim informed them
"I have a few little cancer cells on my brain
Don't worry, but pray for me, all the same."
Jim died bravely, without discovering the answer
To a wonder cure for his insidious cancer
Held by his adopted country in such high esteem
A State Funeral with trimmings was arranged for him
The city stopped and joined in the prayer
Proud of this man whom with Ireland they share
The family confronted a void they could not ignore
Like when he left Ireland two decades before
Jim was dead and that nothing could fix
There was now only five where there once had been six
Jim was gone and through the aching dull pain
Came sad realization he will never phone home again

Julia

Julia Gillard was Australia's first woman Prime Minister and had to endure relentless personal and political attacks purely because she was not a bloke. She endured with dignity, thus making it easier for women who follow.

Woman, smile sweetly while we men insult you
It's just a joke, we love, adore and exalt you
Our words mean no harm, pure political commentary
We love having you around, you're not an adversary
All we ask is that you have the grace
To desist from leadership roles in this place
It's hard for us blokes when you won't toe the line
The Prime Minister should not be a woman, get out now, resign
How dare you assume that you can lead our nation
You're a woman for God's sake, with ideas beyond station
In this country of mateship we've no place at the table
For women, no matter how talented and able
Sexist buffoonery, time and time again
Dished out to women who dare to complain

Radio shock jocks and conservative commentators
Aggressively undermine
Reduce you to concubine
Reinforce inequality through patriarchal structures
That strive to denigrate and define
"Don't play the gender card," a condescending accusation
"Face the fact, you're not up to the task of leading this great nation."
A curious remark applied if a woman dares complain
About the constant misogyny faced time and time again
Small breasts, huge thighs and a big red box on the menu
Is that how most of your male colleagues see you?
You are the first female to lead our nation,
the sitting Prime Minister
Yet they regard you as a bird to bone, how horrible and sinister!
They treat you as a lesser being, and to a quail compare you
You persist on being in the public eye, how dare you
We men, our wit and wisdom, enhanced with intellect and reason
Regard a woman in our world is an act of pure treason
So shut up in public, know your place, get behind us
How dare you come out and remind us
You have a power that you're unaware of
Something profound that we are so scared of
There's a reason we hold females open to scorn
For without women, we men would never be born

Midwinter madness

On the 21st June 2012, the winter solstice, the Australian Parliament voted to bring back offshore detention for refugees, a policy that had been introduced by the previous Coalition Government and found to be grossly inhumane. It was dismantled when the Gillard Labor Government was formed but political pressure had been bought to bear and now the policy that Labor had once despised was being re-introduced with eyes on the polls.
It was a dark day in Australian politics!

Midwinter madness under stormy sky
Inside Canberra's Chambers
Warm and bright
Immovable arguments sully the longest night
Pompous politicians
Labor and Coalitions
Pontificate
Adjudicate
We will decide who comes to this country and why
Our side has might
Always right
Blind adherence to ideology
False premise, sad mythology
Mindless zealots
Trying to tell us
No room for compromise

As under dark skies
Poor souls with no homeland
Abandoned
Hopefully head towards freedom
Dreamland
Terrified but hopeful
Predicament woeful
Waves crash
Hopes dashed
Trauma, disaster, distress
Poor people already dispossessed
Cast aside into the dark deep
Babies drown, grown men weep
As refugees struggle in the cold dark sea
Survivors rescued by naval patrols
Politicians cry crocodile tears and disagree
Through xenophobic eyes on the polls
Good people die while debate rages
The rescued ones are locked in cages
Who will defend the rights of the poor?
Not one politician will cross the floor
While this still happens we must all be blamed
Australia, be very ashamed

Boys will be boys

Every weekend there's mob violence where someone gets hurt
Killer punch delivered, head hits ground, victim inert
A football player out of his mind on drugs and alcohol
The husband who belts his wife, abuses her, calls her moll
Our patriarchal society excuses these things
Says boys will be boys, the "y" chromosome wins
Boys toys, toys for boys
Cars, boats, X-box, anything that makes noise
Talk for boys, boys talk
Who will win the footy, what sheila shall we stalk?
Boys games, war games
What is it about love of war that passion inflames?
Men's business, business for men
We will decide who, what and when
Inside every man there is a little boy
Mother's pride and joy becomes grown playboy
Ever resisting to take his place
As a grown up equal in the human race
How often do we see women hoon around in cars
Dropping doughnuts on the street, getting into fights in bars
Do lady politicians sit up high in huge, black tanks
Or get behind a tommy gun gaily shooting blanks?
Do mothers dream of military might, and strategic war games play
Collect ancient, gruesome weapons and put them on display
Does a female astronaut dream of conquering Mars
Or of inner planetary wars fought amongst the stars
No, women hold none of that dear, they have no time to spare
They are too busy nurturing the next generation in their care
"Boys will be boys," the old and tired excuse
Rolled out to forgive every sin from stupidity to child abuse

Go to Hell, George Pell

Go to hell, George Pell
You let your people down
You didn't serve us well

Be ashamed, George Pell
You protected evil priests
And called victims infidel

The plaintiff bared his soul, George Pell
While not one word you uttered
In the people's citadel

You knew right from wrong, George Pell
Yet moved the bad priests on
To spread their evil spell

You should have sounded the bell, George Pell
But you didn't, instead
Children suffered living hell

Be humble, George Pell
You climbed the ecclesiastical ladder high
It was a long way when you fell

'Fess up, George Pell
If not for what you did
Then because you didn't tell

Suffer little children

Come in, Father
How would you be, Father?
Sit down, Father
Have a cup of tea, Father?
Please bless this house
And everybody within
May we live good lives free from sin
We place you high on your pedestal
Standing above us, knowing it all
Anointed celibate one
Meet my precious son
Who with God's grace may one day become
One of you, what joy that would bring
Make it all worthwhile, all the pain and suffering
So, at the end of life, after this trouble and strife
My ticket is punched
Ensuring heavenly life
Father, would you like some lunch?

Come to Father, little boy
You, an occasion of sin
My sex toy
You made me do it
Made me give in
You are my temptation
Cause of your own violation
Pray, ask forgiveness
For we have sinned, the both of us
My own development was arrested
By a priest whom I detested
Best not tell, stay out of Hell
Don't tell your parents, little boy
They believe in our Church and me
And my vow of celibacy
They know that I would not hurt a flea
They will not believe you, they honour me

Betrayed

A head full of curls and big blue eyes
He commanded attention and got it
He walked the town, always playing the clown
But inside, he was tortured and rotted

Mass, Rosary, prayers and Benediction
The family's religion, a cult affliction
Say your prayers, climb the stairs
Ensure an eternity in Heaven
Heed the priest when he talks, he is revered
And stands at the right hand of God
You spoil the child
If you spare him the rod

So, in this rhythm the good parents lived out their lives
Doing what they thought right and good
What they didn't know then and I'm telling you now
A predator lurked in their 'hood

"Be aware, stranger danger," they had cautioned their child
Bad men can do you great harm."
When right there in their kitchen as their guest of honour
A priest wielded his poisonous charm
Using his collar to groom their young son
Making him his chosen one

The priest cunningly smiled as the child he defiled
"Pull down you pants," he told the young boy
I'll also drop mine so you won't feel uncomfortably coy
I'll show you my dance, as your life I destroy
By my act of buggery, my ultimate thuggery."

"Now it's over let's pray, you tempted me today
Take this holy card and we won't go to Hell
Your rape is our secret, be sure not to tell
Kneel down now and let us pray
God, let our sin be taken away."

A great burden was laid on the boy's young head
As he lay crying in bed, his little bum bled
With no one to turn to, desolate and forlorn
Oh, how he wished he had never been born

His parents noticed the change in him
But knew not the cause
He wanted to tell them
But he couldn't because
Deep down in his heart he knew that they'd rather
Uphold their religion
Than have a bad word said about Father

So alone he kept on, his hurt he kept hidden
Deep in his psyche, where it lay still and raw
His life was a mess, he was cut right to the core
And to speak out was virtually forbidden

For forty years he did his best to go on
Bury that treacherous violation
But he couldn't because it coloured his life
Caused self-hate, despair and degradation
An impossible task, he could bear it no more
His tortured mind convinced him there was absolutely nothing left
to live for

Bless me, Father

Bless me, Father, for I have sinned
And this is my Confession
I am guilty of aggression
Swore once or twice
Wasn't very nice
Complained about the roast
Didn't eat my toast
Didn't say my prayers,
Ran up and down the stairs
Bless me, Father, for I have sinned

I was a happy boy and life was simple
Indoctrinated by priests
Who were God's earthly symbol
Consecrated and venerated
I believed it all
There was no escape
Until that wicked man committed rape
Evil unmitigated, childhood obliterated
Left me broken, all bent and hollow
To suffer life in the years that follow

Son, I have sinned against you,
Abused and raped you
Simply because I could do
Left you nowhere to escape to
While I indulged my sexual fantasy
Sinfully betrayed your family
Led you to a life of insanity
And I did it with impunity
Because you were beholden unto me
Who was ordained to converse with Deity
Not sorry for the pain I wrought
Simply sorry that I got caught

Fuck you, Father, because you have sinned!

Out of options

Exhausted, he can endure no more
Of abuse heaped upon abuse that has gone before
The time comes to stand and succumb
Choose the noose over the gun
Need for peace, no more tears to be cried
The only option left was suicide
The priest made him his toy when he was only a boy
And years later when he complained
He suffered the rape all over again
Justice, compassion and the truth suppressed
His trauma never compassionately addressed
The best lawyers in town were set against him
Loudly called him liar, abused and distressed him
Paid paltry compensation from the Church's vast riches
What happened to practicing what ones preaches?
Instead, silence, a confidentiality agreement
He was shamed and re-abused by this mistreatment
Poor, damaged soul, head hanging in a noose
Murdered by the Church, facilitator of his abuse

Black lives matter

A black man gasping for breath
White policeman kneeling on his neck
I can't breathe, I can't breathe
George Floyd, dead, a victim of racial hatred
A moment of awakening, the hurt translated
To the whole world
In Australia, David Dungay
Gasps for breath in the same way
Several policemen, physically restraining
David helplessly explaining
I can't breathe, I can't breathe
No media attention his death received
Why does this happen? Why do we not grieve?
Australians seem to sympathise
When foreign black men lose their lives
Yet fail to translate this to our situation here
Where aboriginal youth live in constant fear
From the constabulary and similar issues are at play
Yet receive little or no out-cry, no dismay
Australians seem to have less empathy
For our own black deaths in custody
I wonder why would that be?
Is it because they occur in remote corners of the country
Is it much easier to ignore what we do not see
Many Indigenous communities
Wonder where is justice for their families?
It happens on our own doorstep
Young aboriginal men die, and yet
We fail to recognise the cries of anguish and despair
When it comes from over here, and not from over there

ANZAC Day 2020

It's ANZAC Day in lockdown
Flying foxes in their riverside retreat the only sound
As houses slowly waken and there is stirring in our street
And we assemble one by one to stand and commemorate
The brave men and women who have gone before
Who fought and died for our country in many a bloody war
Dogs bark, the neighbour's pet rooster crows
The first morning coffee brews, outside dim light glows
Torches illuminate the dawn
ANZAC Service has come home
Young couple reverently places a candle on the kerb
From various houses young families emerge
A child proudly wearing war medals given long ago
To a man who has gone before that he didn't even know

An Australian flag proudly draped across the gate
A chalk-drawn soldier on the pavement of the house at number eight
Along the street faint glow of candles on the pavement
The simplicity of the gesture a sentimental statement
An old man wears his medals from the Vietnam war
His wife who stands by his side knows who he's crying for
Two nature strip trees decorated with knitted poppies red
The crafty women completed that task before they went to bed
A breeze of muted whispers, as in the background
The distant buzz of motor cars, towards the city bound
The flat note of a child trumpeter in the light of a lamp post
Plays a delightfully imperfect version of the "Last Post"
Two minutes of silence, a time for reflection
Some homemade wreaths laid with reverend circumspection
Then "Reveille" and "Lest We Forget"
ANZAC Day in lockdown, so simple and yet
The sun rises
To another day in lockdown
Full of surprises

Cleaning out the garage

We've done all the household chores, thanks to the coronavirus
The windows are clean, the skirtings gleam, spiders downed from their cobwebs
The curtains are washed, the oven scrubbed, gone is the kitty litter
Floors are polished, silver rubbed so that it shines a light and bright glitter
Cupboards emptied and stacked neatly when cleaned
Not one speck of dust is to be seen
The house is so sparkling but it's only I that know it
I should ask the neighbours in, if only just to show it
I have watched everything and anything on Netflix
Taught the dog a handful of new tricks
Out in the garden, things look shipshape
I've planted out vegies and watch them take shape
The grass is green, the leaves raked up
Paths are so clean, weeds burnt up
The pool is pristine, I catch each leaf before it flutters
I've even had the ladder out and cleared all the gutters
With nothing more that I can do here
In staunch resolve and tremulous fear

I open the garage door
Just one look says it all
I know that there's a car in there
I can't be exactly sure just where
There are tins of paint stacked high from years before
Bikes, I think I counted six or more
There are kiddies' toys from when men were boys
A three-wheeled pram brings back past joys
There's two or three stuffed boxes and all sorts of tape
Camping gear, six hessian bags, a black magician's cape
There's a pile of out-dated newspapers from when the young lad did the round
I now understand why the newsagent ranted when they could not be found
I stand and ponder this pile of shit
And wonder what I will do with it
Some of it is still quite good and I think aloud if I should
Put it all back and drive to Bunnings to buy more shelving
This task at hand is too overwhelming

Summer 2020

Australia's burning, Australia's burning
Fetch the water, fetch the water
What water? There ain't no water!

Fish are dying, fish are dying
Fill their river with water
What water? It's on the cotton crop!

Koalas crying, bandicoots dying
Wash their wounds with water
No water, only koala tears!

Nature is angry, climate is changed
Life on earth needs to be rearranged
Politicians heads deranged
Coal wins
Money is king

Locked out of the sunshine

Our bags are packed, we're off to Queensland
It's too cold here, we're sniffing and sneazlin'
Winter in Melbourne is far too chilly to stay here
We're heading up north where we fritter time away there
Until the sun comes back down to Capricorn
Then it's too hot for comfort so we head back home
The summer clothes have been washed and ironed
The caravan is hooked up, the wheels realigned
The house is clean and the dog is safely in the back
Nothing left to do, nothing left to pack
Hang on
What's this, what's wrong?
The borders are shut, they won't let us through
They don't want Victorians, what are we to do?
They reckon we carry the coronavirus
They've hung us out to dry before they even tried us
I'm as mad as hell, all anger and ire
It's a staycation for us in front of the fire

Groundhog day

I've been locked up, locked down and locked up again
I'm a people person so it's against my grain
But Dan says, "Stay home, work through the pain."
Just to quote the old cliché
It's groundhog day,
Again, again, again, the same

Stay inside, don't venture out, don't leave your floor
Nobody wants to talk any more
Me and my faithful Labrador
Watch statistics mount with dismay
It's groundhog day
Again, again, again, the same

Dan says it's not too much to ask
If you venture out wear a mask
Stealthy figures slink silently past
A bad guy or good guy, I innocently ask?
Can't come out to play today
It's ground hog day
Again, again, again, the same

People dying, mourners crying
If this gets away it will be terrifying
It's essential to have us all complying
People in the churches pray
It's groundhog day
Again, again, again, the same

Stay at home, don't go far, immobilise us
Public shame, a huge fine, a dose of the virus
Police will check credentials

Allow us out to buy essentials
If we falter, we pay
It's groundhog day
Again, again, again, the same

Endless football on the TV
Sit outside in the sun and read
Empty the garden of every weed
Knit a jumper for Uncle John
Another six weeks, it goes on and on and on
In my home hideaway
It's groundhog day
Again, again, again, the same

Now it's all for one and one for all
Let's get this done, what are we waiting for
Third time for real, this is all-out war
Vanish doomsday and groundhog day
If this lockdown proves a failure
Victoria will be the laughing stock of Australia

Other works by Elsie Johnstone

Our Little Town, Growing Up in Lakes Entrance 2009
Lover Husband Father Monster - Her Story 2010
Ma's Garden 2012
Around the Kitchen Table 2012
Rainbow Over Narre Warren 2014
Lover Husband Father Monster - The Aftermath 2015
Lakes Entrance girl - Collected Poems 2020

Portrait of the author as a diligent Catholic Primary School student.

www.ingramcontent.com/pod-product-compliance
Lightning Source LLC
Chambersburg PA
CBHW030303010526
44107CB00053B/1799